The Poetry Catchers

by

The Pupils of Craigton Primary School and Nursery

Augur Press

THE POETRY CATCHERS
Copyright © Craigton Primary School and Nursery Pupils
2008

British Library Cataloguing in Publication Data.
A catalogue record for this book is available from the British
Library.

ISBN 978-0-9549551-9-9

First published 2008 by
Augur Press
Delf House,
52, Penicuik Road,
Roslin,
Midlothian EH25 9LH
United Kingdom

Printed by Lightning Source

The Poetry Catchers

With thanks to Mrs Sandra McCay, a teacher who continues to work tirelessly to inspire creative potential in the school.

Thanks also to all the parents and carers, who gave permission for the children's poems to be published.

Contents

Foreword

Reading poetry is a way of life for Craigton Primary pupils. They even have their own Poetry Lending Library.

Now, with this book, they have become poets themselves! They have 'caught' poems by telling anecdotes, delving into their imagination, and heightening their awareness of the world around them.

One pupil summed it up like this: 'Poetry isn't so hard. All you need are memories.'

This book features a favourite poem from every child in the school, and some from our nursery class too. I am so proud of my Poetry Catchers. They have produced some delightful and thought-provoking poems, and have learned more about themselves and others along the way.

I hope that you enjoy reading the poems.

Kind Regards,

Sandra McCay

Catching poems is easy.
You don't have to think or do.
Just open your heart and your senses,
And the poems will come to you.

Sandra McCay

Nursery

My Favourite Place

Ciaran Hunter
I watch a film. I liked 'A Bear Hunt'.

Ross Douglas
I like to go to Asda crèche because it's got slides.

Reis Thomson
I like to go to my nursery. I like to play with Matthew.

Mason McLeod
Shops. Go with Mum.

Paul Murphy
I like to go to Toys 'R Us. My mum buys me stuff.

Jessica Wright
Asda. I like to play in the Asda crèche. I feel happy.

Max Watt
Toys 'R Us. A big black Buzz Light Year. It's a new one.
I feel great.

Ben Ferguson
Shops. Yes!

George Cooke
To Telly Tubby Park next to a swimming park.
I feel jumpy. My granny lets me roll my eggs down a hill.

Matthew Nisbet
I like Toys 'R Us to see the Ben Ten figures.

1

Scott Campbell
I like going to the park because I like the swings.

Logan McFarlane
My favourite place is nursery because I like the caterpillar.

Lulu Douglas
I like going to my gran's.

Missy Arriola
I like Asda because I buy food.

Kai Leith
I like the beach. I like water and sand. I make sandwiches.

Zak Mersey
Go on holiday with Mummy, Daddy, Kyle, Scott and Ethan.

Nathan Rose
The chippy. To get chips and some fish.

Jack Turner
I like to go to Spain. That's where Daddy's house is.

Elise Cameron
I like going to America to see Minnie Mouse and Donald Duck and Captain Hook.

Harris Leckie
I like to go to Ibiza. Walk down the beach and sometimes swim in the pool.

Molly Duncanson
I like to go with my cousin. I like to go to the park or the beach.

Brogan Nicholson
I like Toys 'R Us to buy bikes.

Rachel Hughes
I like the park.

Ellis Douglas
I like McDonalds. I get chips.

Rozita Swanepoel
I like the park. I play.

Abi Murray
I like my room. I like to play on my piano.

Rory Woods
I like my auntie Susan's. I play with a brown car. When I go
home I take it, then I bring it back.

Adam Patten
I like the park. My dad lets me take my skateboard.

Eve Logan
I like Disney. I cuddled Goofy. He was dressed up like Santa
and he played Jingle Bells.

Olivia Gailey
I like dancing and swimming. I know how to swim in the
baby pool.

Gemma Cumberland
I like dancing because I like to do star jumps.

Glen Patten
Swimming. I swim in the water.

Lennon Brown
I like swimming. I've got a big circle thing that goes round you.

Derek Pickles
I like swimming. I like to jump in the water.

Shirel Like Botende Wa Bokota
I like McDonalds, to get the animals.

Mia McKechnie
I like to go to the café. I get a carton of juice.

Adam Oz
The park. To run.

Steven McKee
I like my dad's house. I tidy up my room. It's a big mess.

Primary One

My Imaginary Friend

He lives on top of the roof.

He comes down at dinner.

He eats lasagne and garlic bread.

He comes to school,

And smacks my teacher's bottom!

Lewis Andrews

Lewis

He has soft hair.

He always shares his play-piece.

We play at tig.

I keep winning.

Ryan Baird

My Imaginary Friend

My imaginary friend is called Sophie.

She lives in my house, in my room.

We play hide and seek.

She likes to eat fish fingers.

Olivia Bell

I was angry

I was angry with my hamster

because he bit me.

Rachel Campbell

Cameron Taylor

He has blonde hair.

He has green eyes.

He has got a smiley face.

He likes Transformers.

Cameron Clark

My Imaginary Friend

She lives in the clouds.

Her name is Sophie.

I talk to her.

I can see her sometimes.

When it's sunny.

Eva Clark

Eva

She has blue eyes.

She has blue bobbles.

She has bunches.

She has a toy.

She has a cardigan.

She has soft skin.

Eve Coffey

My Imaginary Friend

He stays with me.

His name is Tom.

His favourite game is Princesses.

I am the Princess, and he is the Prince.

He marries me.

He sometimes comes down for dinner.

Nadia Coia

My Imaginary Friend

My imaginary friend is in my house.

Her name is Lucy.

I love her.

I play games.

I love her.

'You are my best friend.'

I love her.

She is special

Alicia Debaie

My Sadness

I was sad when my Gran died.

I got to make cakes.

I was really, really sad.

Ruby Dickson

My Imaginary Friend

He's a dog.

He's called Scooby Doo.

He likes to play 'hide and seek'.

He eats my dinner sometimes.

I just keep eating.

He sometimes goes in the garden.

I play 'fetch' with him.

Joseph Gilmour

I was ill

I was sad when I was ill.

I was sick in my bed.

I shouted 'MUM! I've been sick!'

She said 'I'm coming!'

She helped me.

Lisa Haggarty

My Imaginary Friend

My imaginary friend lives with me.

His name is Cat.

I play with him.

I even play with my toy shark with him.

I don't remember what I say to him.

Kelvin Keenan

When I fell at School

I was sad when I fell at school.

I tripped up and fell onto the ground.

My nose was bleeding,

And my knee was cracked.

Then I went upstairs.

Elliot McDermott

The Doll

Once upon a time there was a doll on the toy shelf.
Her hair was black.
And her trousers were black.
And she was loved a lot.

When she was alone she went on an adventure.
She went to the magic pot,
And it flew off.
She was so excited.

She looked out and saw the whole world.
She climbed up in space.
She climbed on the moon,
And ate all the blueberries she could.
And then she went home.

The little girl went in the room.
'Where have you been?' she said.

Nicola McGarrity

Bad Dog

I was angry with my dog,

Because it didn't poo on the newspapers.

It pooed in the kitchen.

I said, 'Go and lie down now!'

Ellie McKenna

Loud Boy

I was angry with my brother,

When he was playing his guitar.

It was too loud.

I said, 'Stop it. You're too loud!'

He said, 'No.'

I went to tell my mum.

She told him not to,

And he STILL didn't stop!

Lucy Milne

My Sister

I was angry with my sister,

Because she wouldn't let me in to her
computer.

I said, 'I'll tell Mum on you!'

She said nothing.

Then she went and told on me.

Mum gave her into trouble.

She said, 'Get off the computer anyway!'

Hannah Mitchell

Me

I like play football.

I like play with my friend Dylan.

I like paint my Daddy, my Mummy, myself.

I like eating bread.

Daniel Okolo

Tom

My imaginary friend likes pizza.

He lives in my room.

I like to play with him.

His name is Tom.

Nathan Quinn

My Imaginary Friend

His name is John.
He likes to play Transformers.
He's very good fun.
He plays what I love on TV.
Scooby Doo and the Werewolf.
Every type of Scooby Doo in the whole
history.
I can only see him.
He sleeps in the cupboard.
He likes chicken.
I come up with his dinner.
I take a chicken drumstick
When my mum's not looking,
And I give it to him.
He's hungry all the time,
Because he only gets one thing to eat.

Marc Rooney

Bedtime

I was angry with my mum

Because I had to go to bed.

She said, 'Now you have to go to bed.'

I said, 'No.'

She said, 'It's time for bed.'

Cameron Taylor

My Imaginary Friend

His name is Tom.

He always plays wrestling,

And he always wins.

He stays in my room,

Sleeping in the morning.

He gets up at night time,

Saying, 'Hello! I'm here in the pub.'

I always say, 'Get back to sleep!'

Dylan Underwood

LiliJade

LiliJade has black hair.

She is pretty.

Ben Wang

My Brother

Jin Peng is my little brother.

We play on the swings together.

He is fat and cuddly.

LiliJade Wang

Primary Two/One

The Naughty Dog

I was happy when my dog was one.

I got mad at him,

Because he was trying to pull my trousers.

I said, 'STOP IT NOW!'

He stopped it.

Cameron Blair

When my Best Friend Doggy died

One day my nana's dog died.

I was sad.

Like never before.

And very upset.

But she's in no pain now,

Because she's up in heaven.

I miss her very, very, very much.

Leigha Brewis

The Day I was Angry

Every day,

My brother pushes me down the stairs.

So I got angry.

I ran up the stairs,

And lifted my big brother.

I threw him down the stairs.

He was crying,

And I was laughing.

So was my Mum.

Adam Fitzpatrick

I was playing

I was playing with my friend.

I pushed him in a puddle.

I said, 'Oh no!'

He pushed me into a puddle.

Then he said, 'Oh no!'

Cameron Greig

The Mad Park Day

One day I went to the park.

It was raining.

I had my wet suit on.

I was rolling about like a dog.

When I got home,

I was dripping wet.

Emma Junnor

35

When Tyson got put down

One day my dog called Tyson,

Got put down.

My mum and gran took him.

I said, 'Can I go?'

My mum said, 'No.'

I started crying,

But I got a cat instead.

Jade Masson

The Water in the Toilets

When I was in P1, I was scared of the toilets

Because I didn't like the flushes in case

the water went up to the top.

Now I am in P2, I use the staff toilet.

Jack McCammon

The Day I was Angry

In the middle of the night,

My wee brother climbed up my ladders,

And jumped up on me.

I jumped down my ladders,

And put him into his bed.

Brandon McGlinchey

I was Angry

I was angry with my cat.

She jumped onto the table,

And she ate my dinner.

I said, 'DON'T DO THAT!'

Lia McGurk

The Megazord

One day I wanted to get my Megazord.

I said to my sister,

'Go and get my Megazord.'

She came downstairs,

With two Power Rangers.

I said, 'Come upstairs with me.'

Then we got my Megazord.

Alexander McKechan

Fudge

One day my dog ran away.

It got out of the back gate

Because it wasn't locked.

I had to go after it.

I had to go on tiptoe,

So my dog didn't hear.

Then I caught it with a collar.

Ellie McMurdo

One day …

One day, I wanted to go to school

But my mum said I was late.

She said that I could stay off.

Then I laughed and said,

'You're not joking, are you?'

'No.'

Then I said, 'Okay.'

Janelle Meikle

The Day my Fish died

Last Saturday my fish died.

I was sad,

Because my mum told me

'One of your fish died.'

Its name was Star.

I put it down the toilet.

Lisa Mullen

Tig

I play with Darren.

We play tig.

Sometimes I get mad,

And run about tigging

EVERYBODY!

John Mwanyali

When Grandma died

One day my grandma died.

We had a special night,

Called 'Fish and Chip' night.

When I went to the funeral

I was five.

My grandma died at her house.

Mia Rafferty

My Imagination Tunnel

I went into the big tunnel and saw lots of lights
It was not dark at all
I came to a place with trees, park and space
I felt surprised
I met a Scorpion with a bin on his back
He gave me spiders with bins on their backs
The spiders collected the rubbish
The last thing he said to me was
You are a Wizard
I said HUH!

Martin Robson

My Imaginary Friend

My imaginary friend

She is called Abbi

She is a girl

We play together.

Hannah Smart

I felt scared

One day I was in the living room

and my Dad was in the shower.

I heard some whistling and no one was there.

I went up the stairs to Dad and I told my Dad.

I waited for him to come out.

I heard footsteps and still no one was there.

I felt scared.

Anni Smith

I was in the shower

One night when I was in the shower

I was singing in there.

I was singing 'It's the season to be jolly!

Fa-la-la-la-la-la la la la!'

Jordan pushed me.

Then I smacked his bottom.

I fell into the glass.

Jack Stewart

Nipping John's Bum

I play with John.
We play together.
John runs about mad
Tying all the people up.
The people nip John's bum.
John runs away shouting
AAAAAAAHHHHHHH!

Darren Whyte

The Scary Dark Tunnel

I went into a scary dark tunnel
I found a way out
I was excited and I was happy.
I saw sand, water and trees
I was on the beach and I saw a Zebra
His name was Ali Bali
Ali Bali gave me a present.
It was a hand.
He said 'I hate you.'
I punched him in the head.

Lee Wright

Primary Two

My Imaginary Friend

My imaginary friend is a cockroach.

My friend likes playing football with me

and its name is Foot Fraction.

And it likes eating octopus with me.

Jennifer Adams

53

Snow

One day I went out in the snow.

I made a snowball.

I threw it at my mum and dad.

Then I threw one at Tommy.

Liam Brown

What makes me happy

I am happy when my mum is cuddling me

and when I am playing with my friends.

Luke Butterfield

When I was playing football

One day I was playing football with my dad.

I kicked the ball in his face.

He fell.

Then I kicked him.

His nose was bleeding.

He said 'aww'.

Jordan Carlin

My Angry Time

I had a fight with my dad.

He tied me in a knot.

Then he let me go.

Then I got a cushion and hit him.

Then I did a 619 on him.

I punched him again.

Callum Coakley

My Imaginary Friend

My imaginary friend is a girl

And her name is Alisa.

She is a very good friend.

Her favourite games are hide and seek and tig.

We have lots of fun together.

She sleeps beside me at bedtime,

And wherever I go she comes with me.

I like her hair because she has blonde hair.

Emma Conaghan

My Dream

One night I was sleeping and I had a dream.

I saw a fox in my dream.

I said, 'Fox, fox, where's the fox?'

Then I found the fox.

A man came and he chased after me.

Then I had cramp and I was crying.

Brandon Copeland

Snowing time

It was snowing.

I threw a snowball at Dylan and Rebecca.

Rebecca fell into the plants.

I ran away from them.

Mum came.

Dylan and Rebecca were grounded for two weeks.

I did not get grounded.

Joirdan Crawford

My Visit to the Dentist

A long time ago I went to the dentist.

He took my tooth out.

I was crying.

When I woke up I was sick on the floor

in the kitchen.

Millie Donnachie

My Holiday

One day I was at my holiday.

I was playing some games.

I had a big breakfast.

I was playing with some of my toys.

Scott Douglas

My Sad Day

One day my pet fish died.

Then my other fish died.

I felt sad.

My mum said, 'Your pet fish died.'

Morgan Flynn

When my mum crashed

When my mum crashed into the pavement,

we went home.

We phoned a taxi.

We went to the hairdresser's.

My mum got a haircut.

I went to the shops beside the hairdresser's.

When we came back we had dinner.

My mum's car is now fixed.

Ajay Green

The Rabbit in the Tunnel

On my journey I went into a very
big dark tunnel
I met a fluffy rabbit
I felt very happy
The rabbit ran away
He came back
I took him home with me
It was a great day.

Robbie Hughes

When I was playing on the computer

One day, on the Nintendo Wii,

I could not beat Kyle at the javelin throwing.

I put it onto the racing,

And I got a new world record.

I said, 'Yes!'

Ryan Hunter

My Wrestling-match

I had a wrestling fight with my dad.

He would not let me play my Wii.

I hit him and I did an RKO on him.

Then I punched him.

He said 'Shut up' to me.

Then I could play my Wii.

Ciaran Kane

She aged 6

My eyes are green.

My nose is small.

It does not have many freckles.

My lips are red.

I wish all the boys would go away.

Katey Kerr

My Fight

One day I had a fight with my friend.

I jumped on him.

Then he did a six on me.

I told my mum.

William Marr

My Imaginary Friend

My imaginary friend is a boy.

He has a big top and blue eyes and red trainers

and I like him.

David McCluskey

A Chalk Fight

One day I had a chalk fight with Brandon's sister.

I said 'Ha ha ha ha!'

She said, 'I will chase you round the room.'

She put chalk on me.

I was angry.

We were playing schools.

I was the teacher.

Danielle McCracken

My Fight

One day I had a fight with my brother.

I punched him in the knee.

I punched him in the jaw.

I punched him in the teeth.

I kneed him.

I bit him.

He punched me.

Then my mum came in.

I was grounded for punching him in the teeth.

I couldn't play pool.

Max McRae

My Gran

One day my gran died.

I was sad.

She died at the hospital.

She went up to heaven.

So I am going to the church every Sunday,

So I can talk about my gran.

Lucy Millar

My Granda

My Granda died with cancer.

I can't remember what he said to me.

He could not walk.

He could not eat.

I was very sad.

Nicole O'Toole

I made a Snowman

Last Saturday it was snowing.

I made a little snowman.

Then it melted.

I was sad.

I went home,

And my mum took a picture of the snowman.

Ryan Oz

My Angry Time

I had a fight with my big sister.

I kicked her, and I said 'Go to your room.'

'I won't go to my room' she said.

So I punched her, and kicked her again.

Then I slapped her on the face.

And I kicked her again.

Jordan Reid

The Snow

When it was snowing

I jumped on my dad's snowman.

Then I threw a snowball at my dad.

Then I pulled his hat over his eyes.

He fell in the snow.

He had a cold.

Shaun Robertson

When I went to the Football

One afternoon I went to the football.

There was a big puddle.

I got soaked.

I was angry.

I was growling.

Ben Slater

My Snow Angel

It was snowing.

I asked if I could make a snow angel

But my mum said no.

But my uncle Alistair said yes.

I said to my mum 'Ha ha ha.'

So I made an angel and a snowman.

Hollie Slater

Snow

On Saturday I went out in the snow.

I went to make a snow angel.

My jacket was ripped.

My mum was going to work.

I threw a snowball at her.

She said, 'I'm going to work!!!'

Emma Whiteside

Primary Three

Me

My gums are pink and hard.

My cheeks have hairs.

I have hairs in my nose.

I have lumps on my gums.

There are people in my eyes.

I do not like school.

I like Christmas and my birthday.

I wish I had a puppy.

Joshua Bailey

Fairies

I have lots of imaginary friends.

My two favourites are Danny and Daisy.

We love to play tig.

The thing I like about them is that they are fairies.

They sleep in mushroom beds.

They live in mushrooms too.

Chantelle Buckley

Me

My ears are soft.

My eyebrows are very bendy.

If I breathe enough I can use my mouth.

My lips are dry and soft.

I like crisps and sweets

but I don't want my teeth to fall out.

Ryan Chicoine

My Face

My eyelashes are black.

My nose has a red mark on it.

My mouth has hair around it.

I wish I was rich.

I hate when I cut my knee.

I want a PS3.

Dylan Crawford

The Shows

One day me and my family were at the shows.

We won two teddies by doing the lottery

with these numbers – 2, 4, 6, 8.

Then we went on the dodgems.

We had great fun.

The best thing was I was with my family.

Lee Devine

All about Me

I have blonde hair and it is quite long.

My earrings are gold

and they are shaped like a loveheart.

My lips are quite soft.

My skin is quite tanned.

I like playing with my friends.

I don't like when me and my friends fall out.

I wish I could ride my bike.

Brooke Docherty

My Journey

I walked down lots of stairs.

It was dark.

I came out at the desert.

I saw a cactus.

I felt great.

I met a rabbit.

He gave me a chocolate bunny.

I gave him a cake.

He said, 'See you another time.'

I walked up the stairs.

Liam Docherty

The Fight

One day me and my little brother

were playing in my room.

My little brother stuck the middle finger up at me.

I told my mum.

My mum said 'Stop being a grass and go back and

play with your little brother.'

So I *marched* back into the room and hit him.

I felt absolutely fantastic again.

Chloe Duncan

The Football

One day I went to the football.

When I was in goals,

someone hit me on the privates.

I shouted 'OUCH!'

My Dad said 'Free kick!'

I said 'Whoever hit me on the privates is in for it!'

When I found out who it was,

I hit them back on the privates!

I said 'Nae joy, loser!'

Lee Duncanson

Me

I have red gums.

I have blonde hair.

I have a yellow nose.

I have blue eyes and black eyebrows.

I like going to the park.

Lewis Fair

Truth or Dare

One day I was playing truth or dare

in the street with my sister.

It was her shot.

My sister dared me to pull my top up and I did!

I did it when an old man passed by!

He put his hand over his mouth

and said 'OH MY GOD!'

He ran as fast as he could!

I said to my sister Colette

'I WILL GET YOU FOR THIS!'

Laura Gibbons

When my Mum goes out

When my Mum goes out
She always wants to look nice.
She says 'Jamie-Lee does this look nice?'
I say 'Yes',
So I can go to bed.
My Mum says 'This doesn't match!'
I go walking into my bed. Zzzzz.
Then she comes into my room and says
'Jamie-Lee! Wake up!'
She drags me out of bed.
I say 'Mum, GET OFF! You look nice!'
I go back to bed.

Jamie-Lee Gillan

My Sister's Baby

My sister has a baby doll.

It's just like a real baby.

She is cute and cuddly.

She had a giraffe dress

and her favourite animal is a giraffe.

My Mum thinks she is ugly.

But I think she's cute.

My sister's boyfriend is her Dad.

She is practising to be a Mum.

Robyn Kennedy

93

My Journey at the Beach

One day I went to Bellahouston Park.
I walked down lots of stairs.
I saw some people.
I came out of a door and ended up at a beach.
I saw water and I felt excited.
I met Gorjer the gorilla and Gorj the monkey.
They gave me a cake and a clown.
I gave them a toy each.
Then I said I was going to go
And they said 'We'll see you at home.'
I went back up the stairs.
My Mummy said 'Where have you been?'
I said 'I have been playing hide and seek.'

Mika Lewis

My Journey

One day I was at the park.
I saw a door. I pulled the door.
I walked down lots of stairs.
I came out at fun world.
I said 'What in the world!'
I went in and said 'Look at all the slides!'
I saw a girl. She said 'Hi I'm Claire.'
Claire had a present for me.
It was tickets to 'Hairspray'.
Suddenly I felt something in my pocket.
It was flowers for Claire.
I said 'Have a good time.'
My Mum said 'Where have you been?'

Cara McFarlane

Dog and Fox Fight

My dog was fighting with a fox.
The fox didn't know what to do.
I shouted for my Mum and said to her
'Mum! Gus is fighting with a fox!'
My Mum said 'Gus, get in the house!'
He went up the stairs.
We thought he was coming in the house,
But he went on the decking.
Eventually he came into the house.
The fox didn't come in my garden.
He went in my next-door neighbour's garden.

Chloe McGinty

Dancing

Once went when I was two.
My mum took me dancing. It was the show.
It was my shot to dance.
I went out and started to dance.
My shot was over and the curtains came down.
My head got stuck in the curtains!
The audience were giggling and laughing.
It was so embarrassing!

The next dancers came on
And my head was still stuck!
The next dance began.
I was heaving to get my head out.
Finally I got my head out.
I had to walk through the other people.
They were all looking at me!
I kept saying it wasn't my fault
Because I was only TWO!

Jennifer McNulty

The Bunny Game

One day my cousin Kerry came over.

It was almost time for Kerry to go home.
I said 'Let's play the bunny game.'
Kerry said 'You're a genius Claire!'
I said 'Thank you Kerry.'
I went downstairs to tell Mummy.
'Mum?'
'Yes?'
'Kerry said I was a genius!'
'How did that happen?'
'Well we didn't know what to play.'
I said 'Let's play the bunny game!'
My mum said 'Wow!'
I went back to play.

Claire Neeson

My Scary Trip

I walked down lots of stairs.

It was dark and scary.

I came out at a door.

I saw lots of trees.

I felt scared.

I met a reindeer.

She gave me a necklace.

I said 'Goodbye!'

Julieann Revie

When my Mum was angry with me

One day my Mum was mad with me.

She put me in my room.

I put my toys on my bed.

My Mum came in my room.

I was putting my toys away.

She said 'I put Courtney to bed.'

I went to my Mum and Dad's room.

I had fun.

I was happy.

Craig Riddell

When Iain got stuck in the toilets

One day, me, my Mum and my big brother Iain
went out for dinner.
Iain went to the toilets.
He got stuck in the toilets.
I went in and Iain was shouting 'Get me out of this
place!'
So I started to hit the door.
Then I opened the door.
Iain said 'How did you do that?'
I said 'Because I was hitting the door, Dumbo!'
'I will start to hit you!' I said.

Jennifer Rielly

Sarah

My nose has hair on it.

My mouth is big.

My tongue had lots of cuts on it.

My skin is peach.

My teeth are bad.

I wish my teeth were good.

I wish my mouth was small.

Sarah Robertson

My Journey

I went to Bellahouston Park.

I saw a door.

I went in the door.

I saw my Mum and Dad.

They gave me a Transformers toy.

I gave them a puppy.

Adam Stewart

Primary Four/Three

Nintendo Wii

I got my Nintendo Wii three days ago.
Billy, my uncle, got it.
I was playing it all day.
I was playing Wii Sports.
My favourite is baseball.
I was playing it myself
Because my little sister doesn't like baseball
And she doesn't know how to play it.
I won.
I felt good.

Liam Bentley

Make-up Woman

One night I got up and went into my brother's room.
I growled, 'Ryan, wake up! The make-up woman is here
to get you!'
He woke up and said 'It must have been a bad dream.'
He went back to sleep.
I jumped on his bed and grabbed my make-up kit.
I took out my lipstick and put it on his lips.
I put blusher on him.
He woke up in the morning.
My Mum said 'Ryan why are you all make-up?'
Ryan said 'I am not a make-up man.'
He went over the mirror.
He screamed.
'AHHHH!! MY FACE!!'
I said 'Pretty, pretty boy!'
He said 'It was the make-up woman.'
I said 'Oh please. There is nothing like the make-up
woman.'
'Hurry up, you two. You're going to be late.'

Taylor Bourke

Snake on my Arm

One day it was my birthday.
A person called Animalman came.
It was a lady.
She brought a snake.
My sister shouted 'GO ON GRAN!'
So she did.
Next it was my turn.
She put it up my arm.
I was HORRIFIED!
She said 'Don't worry.
Paprika (the snake's name) isn't poisonous.'
She tried, but he didn't come out.
She said 'He won't come out!'

Jack Boyle

Lazy Me

One day I came in from school.

I took my shoes off and left them on the floor.

I took my jacket off and put that on the floor.

I turned the TV on and lay down on the couch.

My Mum shouted 'PICK YOUR CRISPS UP!'

I said 'In a minute!'

'NO!' said my Mum.

'Okay' I said.

But I never did.

Andrea Brodie

What I look like

My name is Erin.
My eyes are shining and watering.
I feel like I am in a swimming pool.
My hair is soft.
I feel like I am on a soft cloud.
My mouth is dry.
I feel like the sun is shining on me.
My ears are very soft.
I like my wee hamster Jake.
I don't like cucumber.
I wish I was a singer.

Erin Brodie

The Holidays

Last Wednesday on the holidays
I went to my friend's house.
We played pool for ages.
Finally we stopped for a rest.
Two seconds later we started again!!
I said 'Please stop.'
He said 'Okay.'
I said 'Thank you very much.'
We watched the telly for about half an hour
And then we played pool again.
About an hour later we went out to play.
Then we got into an argument
That turned into a stone fight.
We found giant stones.
I accidentally missed him.
I was so lucky.
He missed me.
In the end we made up.
After that I went home.

Bez Brown

Me and my brother fight

One morning I was going to my Gran's house.

When I got there my big brother started to fight with me.

I was crying. I shouted to my Mum.

She shouted at him. 'Don't do that!'

Stephanie Bruce

The Christmas Present

When it was Christmas I gave my Mum a present.

It wasn't from me but she opened it.

She dropped it.

She thought it was a bar of soap.

It was a watch.

Then she saw it and she said 'Oohhh!'

Emma Collins

When I got a fright

One night I was sleeping and I heard a noise.

I woke up.

I screamed and I went into my Mum's room.

I screamed.

My Dad screamed.

And we were all screaming.

My Dad stopped screaming and said

'It's probably the old woman next door.'

James Crone

Me

My name is Chelsea.

My eyes remind me of raindrops.

My hair is brown and blonde.

I have freckles on my face.

My eyebrows are light brown.

My hair is soft.

I like my hair soft.

I don't like it when my hair is tuggy.

I wish I was fast.

Chelsea Douglas

The Fight

One day the class was going to gym.
My friends were fighting at gym
because Erin was going to tell the teacher something.
The teacher said to me and Erin
'You can go at the back of me if the ball goes past me.'
Andrea thought the teacher was talking to her.
Andrea went up and did it.
Erin had to sit down.
I said to Andrea 'Why don't you give Erin a shot?'
Then they got back together.

Jade Fisher

The Frog

One day in my old house,
me and my sister Beth were carrying on.
We put a dress on my frog Tago.
He fell down the back of the radiator.
I said 'Oh no!'
'Abby don't you dare tell Dad
or I am going to rip your head off!' Beth warned.
Dad heard something.
He came into the room.
As soon as Beth and me heard Dad we said nothing.
Dad said 'Come on girls. Show me.'
We showed him.
He went bananas.
But then we got him out with a certificate.

Abby Glass

Living in Poland

When I was living in Poland,

My Dad was angry at my Mummy.

My Daddy was no good for my Mum.

My Dad moved house.

We don't have money.

We went to Scotland.

Now I have a Step-dad.

He is good for me and my Mum.

But sometimes I cry for my Dad.

Weronika Jaworska

Me

I saw stars in my eyes.

I saw freckles on my nose.

My hair is smooth.

My ears remind me of a rainbow.

I like juice.

I don't like brussel sprouts

I wish I was at the swimming pool.

Riona Kelly

The Mummy

One night I was in bed and Aidan was too.

I made a noise of a Mummy.

Aidan screamed. He said to me 'A Mummy Dylan!'

'Oh, I don't want this going on again' I said.

'There are no such things as Mummies, Aidan.'

In the morning Aidan said to my mum 'I saw a Mummy.'

'Don't be silly Aidan' said my Mum.

Dylan Langfield

The Day my Guinea Pig went to the Vet

One day my Guinea Pig Tootsie had a fit.
My Mum had to take her to the vet.
I was crying.
She asked me to come with her but I said 'No.'
It was too sad.
When she got back she was wrapped in a towel.
My Mum was holding some medicine.
I asked 'Is she okay?'
My Mum said 'Not really.'
I was really upset.
The next day we had to send her to a Guinea Pig farm.

That was the last time I saw her.

Rosie Murphy

Jerry and the Coke

One day we let our gerbils out of their cage.

One was called Stuart and one was called Jerry.

Jerry had a sniff of my mum's Coke.

Jerry climbed up the glass and SPLASH!!!!

He fell right in.

Corey Thomson

Granny up in Heaven

One day my dad said to me,
'Granny is up in heaven.'
I was sad.

'Is Granny really up in heaven?'
'Yes,' said my dad.
I said 'Can I go and see Granny?'
'Yes, Alan.'
'Thank you.'
So we went to the graveyard.
I was really happy because I was with my granny.

Alan Wright

Primary Four

She aged 8

Hates her little brother
Loves Mrs McCay because she is very nice
Has really light hair
Has long eye lashes

Loves going bowling
Goes to the park after school
Loves dancing
Loves poetry because it is fun
Loves jewellery
Loves Rangers
Loves movies
Loves when her mum goes crazy

Sophie Brown

The Magical World

The tunnel is dark, with solid brick walls.
I saw a little door.
I went in the door.
It was a forest with birds, butterflies, deer and lots more.
I saw a big lake with nice blue water.
Then I saw someone coming to me.
She was carrying a big box.
She said, 'This is for you.'
I took the present off her.
I opened it up.
It was a beagle pup.
Suddenly, I had a box in my hand.
I gave her it and she opened it up.
It was a ruby.
She said, 'My name is Michelle.'
'Bye,' I said. 'Bye.'
I walked away.

Ashley Bryce

Rainbow

I have a teddy called Rainbow.

She is snow white in colour.

I said, 'Mum, can you put a new battery in Rainbow?'

She said, 'Yes, Emma, I will.'

Rainbow lit up lots of beautiful colours.

Red, yellow, pink, green, orange and purple and blue.

Just like the rainbow in the sky.

Emma Clark

Camping on Islay

Finally the summer holidays.
I started singing.
Oh yeah, oh yeah
I'm camping on Islay
Oh yeah, I'm going to Islay.
Then I got tired of singing
So I went to the living room
And watched TV.
I was watching American Dragons.

Four weeks later…
Finally on Monday me and my family
We're going to Islay.
I had no idea where I was going.
When I got there I was amazed.
Days passed and soon it was time to go.
But it was fun.

Sam Conaghan

Animals

I went through a dark tunnel.
When I got down,
there were lions and lionesses with cubs.
There was a small brown door.
I opened the door and I couldn't believe my eyes.
There was lots of grass and a squiggly lake.
There were monkeys, dinosaurs and palm trees.
There was a girl that I thought I knew for ages.
She had a black box in her pocket.
She gave me it. I opened it.
There was a necklace with a tiger.
I felt something in my pocket.
I gave it to her.
When she opened it,
there was a thick piece of glass with a 3-D lion.
She said to me 'Just to remember me by.'

Rebecca Crawford

Murder

One day I went to After School.
We were going on a trip to the woods.
I was wanting to play hidey-tig with my friends.
We went in and started.
Suddenly we stopped.
We saw a knife, a hat, blood
and a tee-shirt amongst the trees.
Suddenly I tripped over a twig
my knee started bleeding.
We ran screaming and found the adults.
They said 'You have split your knee.'
We thought someone was murdered.

Jay Devine

Robert in Mum's Clothes

Mum! Come on.
Hurry up with dinner!
If I were you I'd be much faster.
Want to bet?
Fine then.

I went to the wardrobe.
I dressed up in some of Mum's clothes.
I looked pretty weird.

Mum said 'You want to be me?'
I said 'That's what I'm doing.'
Mum said 'Go and clean the bathroom!'
'I'M NOT DOING THAT!'

Robert Dickson

The Day I got Roco

When Gromit died
It was just too much.
I had to get a new Guinea pig
I got a black and white one!
I named him Roco.
When I got home I started making silly noises
like 'Wooboo Wooboo.'
I was so happy.

Thomas Fenion

Santa's Grotto

A few days ago we had a wet play.
It was really a normal wet play
until Ben MacDonald sat on a chair.
When he sat on that chair
I jumped on his lap and said
'Santa, I want a toy for Christmas.'
Ben said 'YAY!!! I'm Santa
and I'll tell you what you'll get for Christmas.
Since you weigh a … TON …
I'll give you a ticket to the Weight Watchers.'
So it began …
Ben became Santa Claus.
I told Robert about Ben and he said
'Yay! Santa's here!'
So he ran over to Ben and jumped on to his knee and said
'Santa! I want a racing car, a dumper truck and a JCB.'
Ben shouted to Robert 'Get Off Me!
You weigh a TON TOO!'
He threw Robert off his knee
and onto the floor.

Jamie Fitzpatrick

The Bath

One night when I was young
and my dad was putting me in the bath
I forgot to take off my socks … So did my dad.
I thought my sock was my facecloth.
I was going to rub my face with it.
Then I saw it was my SOCK.
I told my mum and dad about it.
Now my mum always puts me in the bath.

Natasha Frate

The Snooze

One day my wee brother Ryan was snoozing in the house
I went up to him
His snoring sounded funny
I started to laugh like mad
I ruined my secret surprise
My wee brother woke up
He said 'Who … who's there?'
I said 'Oopsies! Busted!'
He chased me down the stairs
Then he chased me back up the stairs
I was a bit faster
I had more time
I jumped into his bed
He looked at the lump on his bed
He said 'TIRANAMO!!!!!!!!!'

Kyle Hunter

When my Dog died

When I was coming home from Aberfoyle
I got a McFlurry out of McDonalds.
My mum told me 'SLOW DOWN!!!'
So I speeded up.
She told me that my dog had died.
I started to cry.
My cousin said to her friend to say my dog's name
Just to upset me.
I started crying again.
She wanted me to remember my dog, Mora.
I dreamed about her that night.
So I prayed and prayed for another dog.
My mum said 'You're not getting another dog.'
I *still* prayed for another dog.

Blair Leckie

He aged 8

Has a big cut on his head
Has a bit of black on his nose
Loves Rangers
Hates when Rangers loses
Has a bit of blonde in his hair
Has lots of hairs up his nostrils
Hates Celtic
Loves staying in bed
Hates his cousins
Loves drama
Hates getting told what to do!

Ben McDonald

William died

One day I was on holiday.
I was in Bulgaria when all this happened.
My aunt phoned my mum and she was crying.
Mum said, What is it?
William died.
He died.
Can you tell the kids?
Okay said Mum.
What is it?
You're crying.
Your uncle William died.
I was on the plane going home.
All I did was cry.

Chloe McLean

My Feline Friend

It's name's Diamond
It's a cat.
Scared of noises
How about that?
She's a female, nice and polite
Never gets into fights
And that is right.
I will look after her with all my strength and might.
When I look at you
You look heavy but you are EXTREMELY light.
She has never hurt me, not a bite.
That's my Diamond
ALRIGHT!!!!!

Karen McSporran

Chocolate All Over

One day when I was at Bellahouston Ski Centre
I got Hot Chocolate
when I was watching the freestyle slope.

I fell back.
I spilled it all over me.

So I screamed.
It was burning like hell.

Kyle Mersey

Exploding Purse

On the day of my wee sister's birthday
I gave her a purse.
Then she started to steal money
From my mum and dad.
Then a week later her purse was so big
Because of the money she stole
From my mum and dad.
Then Bang!
The purse exploded.
'I spent a fortune on that purse.
Now you blew it up!'
So I never trusted her with a purse again.

Zac Murray

She aged 8

Has long hair
 Has blue eyes
Has a long fringe
 Has long eyelashes
Loves going to her gran's
 Has lots of toys
Loves sleeping
 Has to try and put up with her brothers saying her name
at bed time
 Hates tomatoes
Has three wee brothers
 Has brown hair
Has a best friend called Rebecca
 Loves to make the dinner and do the dishes
Has had eight teeth out
 Has three squinty teeth
Has glasses to wear until her eyesight gets better
 Has to go swimming with her brothers.

Robyn Patten

My Dog died

One day my dog Sam was walking along
I was watching him
He ran away
I shouted 'SAM!'
He jumped up
He frightened me
We went home
I got his two toys into the garden
We ran about the garden
We went inside
We went into my bedroom
I jumped on my bed
Sam jumped on my bed too
The window was open
I went down the stairs
Sam jumped out of the window
I came upstairs
Sam was gone
I was very sad
I said 'Oh NO! He has jumped out the window.'
He was lost
He *never* came back home.

Lauren Rooney

The Bite

One day when me and my brother
were playing football on my trampoline
OF COURSE I WAS WINNING!
I fell
I had the ball
My brother wanted the ball
I wasn't going to give him it
He BIT me
I shouted
'MUMMM!'
She came out
I said 'HE BIT ME!!!'
My mum smacked him and put him to bed.

Jordan Rose

World Wrestling Loo

One day I was at wrestling.
I was there with my cousin, my dad and my mum.
We were 100th in line.
Then we got to 5th.
'I need the loo.'
'Don't go now.'
'I have to.'
'Hurry up.'
I got back.
'There is no cutting.'
'I was there.'
'Security.'
'If you cut you go to the back of the line.'
'WHAT!'
We got to the end.
'I need the loo.'
'Hurry up.'
'We got 15th.'
'Hey, you don't cut.'
'I was there.'
'Security.'
'You skip, you go to the back of the line.'
'What?'
We got to the end of the line.
We got first.
We got to meet the wrestlers.
We were going home.
'I need the loo.'
'Nooooooooooooooooooo!!!'

Ben Thomson

Boots the Cat

One day I was going to my friend's house
for her birthday party.
I was the first one to notice that Boots the cat was gone.
We looked all over the house for him.
Then my dad said 'I have found Boots.'
'He was in the car all the time,' my dad said.
We took Boots out of the car.
Ten minutes later, Rachel was spinning Boots in her room.
That was because my dad said
'There's no room to swing a cat in here.'
'No, Rachel!' shouted Rachel's mum.

Charlene Topping

Snowball

One day after school my dad took me to the pet shop.
When I had a look at the cats and kittens,
I saw a cute kitten.
I said 'Can I have that one?'
My dad said 'Yes you can have him!'
We took him home.
We named him Snowball.
We got a newer cooler bowl for him.

Karis Watson

Primary Five

The Magic Office

I was in the park with Kayleigh.
I saw a big brass doorknob in the grass.
I opened it and saw a spiral staircase going ...

DOWN
and
DOWN
and
DOWN.

Finally I saw a wooden door with a giant handle.
I opened it and was in an office.
I saw an oak wooden desk set with papers all over it.
Suddenly a thin man with crazy white hair came out of
nowhere.
He gave me red liquid.
I gave him a bottle of green sparkly water.
As he watched me go, he said, 'Thank you!'
When I got back, no time had passed.
It was still two o'clock.
WEIRD!

Rachel Austin

Delia

At the beginning of November
my mum bought me two guinea pigs.
They are called Delia and Fifi.
After a few days,
Delia's eyes were getting crusty and very dry.
We took her to the vet.
She told us to bathe her eyes in cold water.
Soon her eyes were cleared
and we thought she was back to her old self.
Delia was eating a lot and drinking,
and there was no sign that she was not feeling well.
Every night I would sit and watch her play
and run like a mad man on the floor with her sister Fifi.
On New Year's Day my mum came down the stairs crying.
'What's wrong?' I asked her, worried.
'I am sorry,' she said. 'Delia has just died.'
I burst out crying and ran up the stairs to see her.
There she was, lying all stiff and lifeless on my pillow.
The next day we put her in a plastic tub
and buried her around my back garden under a tree.
There is one thing I know for sure,
I will always miss her
and love her deeply in my heart forever and ever.

Lauren Baird

He aged 9

Has grey-blue eyes.
Hates doing work, especially handwriting and reading poetry.
Has blonde, brown hair.
Loves playing games.
Loves Saturday.
Has dark lips.
Loves pizza.
Hates brothers.
Has a sense of humour.
Hates the teachers.
Feels happy when with friends.

Ross Barr

Poetry Poems

Once I was so sad
because I didn't have a poem to write.
I MEAN I WAS SO ANNOYED!!!
I was DRAMATICALLY FURIOUS!!!
I was saying to myself, 'Come on! You can do it.
You can think of a poem.'
Oh good, (say in a silly voice) 'I've got a POEM!'

Johanna Blackie

My Imaginary Friend

When I was a little boy,
I had an imaginary friend called Dan.
He was the best friend in the Universe.
We always played hide and seek.
But it was hard to find him. But he turned up for dinner.
His favourite dinner was ghost spaghetti with coke.
When I came back from my day of school,
He left a note saying,
'My days are over. I will see you in heaven.'
I started to cry.

I grew up, and was in primary five.
I was in the middle of Mrs McCay's writing class
And he came back!
I felt happy.
He plays football with me.
He picks me up from school.

Joshua Campbell

My Imaginary Friend

One day I went to a park.
I went to play on the grass.
When I was running about,
I heard a little shouting voice.
It was coming from under the grass.

So I walked over and I saw a little handle.
I pulled the little handle,
And I fell down a big hole.
I ended up on a spiral staircase.
I went walking down the stairs,
When I fell into an old door.

When I opened the door,
I was in my granddad's attic.
So I had a walk around.
Just then I saw a bright light.
I said, 'Who is that?'
And a little person appeared.

She said, 'I'm Bella's sister.'
(Bella is my old imaginary friend.)
She gave me a stone.
I gave her a flower.
She said, 'Can I be your friend?'
I said, 'Yes.'
We lived happily ever after.

Nicole Cumberland

He aged 9

Has a diamond earring.
Hates football.
Loves swimming.
Feels angry when his family takes things
Without asking.
Has blue eyes.
Loves going boxing.
Has freckles starting from his cheek
To his other one.
Has a good sense of humour.
Feels happy when he's playing with his friends.
Loves maths.
Hates religious studies.
Likes his friends.
Likes Mrs Park and Miss Coyne.

David Duncan

The Day my Guinea Pig fell down

My mum took my guinea pig out.
My two guinea pigs are called Shaggy and Nibbles.
Nibbles came out of my room.
He was at the stairs.
Then my dad came to go down the stairs.
But Nibbles was so frightened he fell
Down the stairs.
He fell down one,
Then he jumped three stairs.
I was so scared.
In the end it was fine.
My dad was crying because he did not know
Me and Thomas were laughing.

Harry Fenion

She aged 9

Has brown eyes.
Loves her Mum and Dad.
Hates her big, fat, ugly, mean sister.
Feels happy when her friends are having a good time.
Feels sad when she thinks of her Papa and Blackpool.
Feels angry when her big sister always gets her own way.
Has a good Best Friend.
Loves nature.
Has a spot on her right cheek.
Has a scar up above her lip.

Nicola Garty

Bye bye Aunty Jean

Last year my Aunty Jean was in hospital.
I think she had a bad illness.
My brother, my Mum and my Dad visited her every Saturday.
When I went to Germany she was still in hospital.
Me and my brother decided to get her a present.
I got her a furry seal.
My brother got her a cat ornament made with real fur.
When we came back from Germany
I wondered if she was okay.
A few days later we gave her the presents.
Two weeks later my Dad was away
because the hospital phoned him.
I came downstairs. My Mum said,
'I'm sorry but Jean died.'
I didn't say anything.
I just cried.

Andrew Hannah

The Day I fooled my Sisters

One day I had a plan to fool my sisters.
I went in and said to them, 'What are you doing?'
One said, 'I'm doing my homework.'
It was time for my plan.
I pushed her head on her homework.
My other sister Limara came over and pushed me to the door,
And tried to push me out …
But I was too strong.
I pushed her away from me.
She got me out.
Then I fell down the steps.
Limara saw me and I pretended I was hurt.
They brought me in.
Then I … Attacked.
They got me out again.
Limara was holding the door.
I pushed it open.
Limara was on the ground, so I
Ran away.

Euan Hill

The New Bed

At my Dad's house I have a room.
I didn't have a bed in my room,
So I got one.
It was meant to come at ten o'clock in the morning.
Instead it came at ten o'clock at night!
Me and my Mum said we couldn't be bothered to take it
upstairs.
When it was in the living room,
I just had to jump on it.
I got a sleeping bag and put it on.
The bed didn't come with covers on it!

Sophie Horne

Calum's Friends

I tripped when I was in the park.
Then I saw that there was a ring in the ground,
And then I realised that it was a door.
And then I opened the door.
I went down the stairs.
I was in a big dark tunnel.
And then I kept walking but there was no way out.
Then I saw a door.
And then I opened that door.
And then I came out onto a beach with sea, sand and nothing
else.
I waited for a minute.
Then my friend Exelarate
Gave me a present.
And it was a quad bike!
And I gave him a present.
It was balls for his feet.
As I was returning to the door he said 'Thank you.'

And one other day I went back and I met another friend –
Booster X 10.
And he gave me an ear piece so I can hear what they are
saying.
I gave him a friend like him except it was a girl.

Calum Kerr

Look closely

It was a gorgeous day and I was in the park.
Suddenly I fell and saw a door.
So being my curious self I opened the door.
The door led me down a dark tunnel,
but at the end there was a colourful splodge.
I walked through the splodge.
Now this is interesting. I saw another door.
I opened the door and ended up in the sky.
I decided to sit on a cushion of cloud, and as I did so, a black
panther with roses and ribbons on its head came up to me and
gave me a tiara and a necklace.
Then I gave the panther a dress with hearts on it.
I was just about to leave when the panther said
LOOK CLOSELY.

Luka Lewis

Weird Place

I was walking in my house.
I saw a door.
When I opened it
I saw a big smelly tunnel.
I walked down the old stairs
Until I saw an old door.
I opened the door
And saw a giant beach.
Someone said, 'Ryan!'
I said, 'Who is it?'
The person walked towards me.
It was my imaginary friend Slyther.
He gave me chocolate.
I felt my pockets and I gave him more chocolate.
Before I left, he said, 'Am I allowed to come?'
I said, 'Yes.

Ryan Lynch

She aged 9

Has blonde silky hair, has sapphire-blue eyes.
Felt sad when she got bullied, hates spiders.
Loves to sing.
Has horrible grey bags under her eyes.
Has the moon shining in her eyes.
Felt worried when she got a detention.
Loves horses.
Felt excited when she was going to the Big Adventure.
Has an annoying dog and big sister.
Hates taking her dog for a walk.
Loves moving her head from side to side when the song
'What is love' plays on the CD.
Loves to sing, 'I like to move it, move it.
I like to move it, move it. I like to move it … you like to …'
But the most important thing is that she's happy
saying a poem in front of the class.

Megan MacDonald

Lola and Tootsie

When Elmo my guinea pig died, I was so upset.
But when my Mum told me that I could get two new ones,
I cheered up.
On the 20th of February 2008 we went to the pet shop
and got two adorable guinea pigs.
I saw two that I had my heart set on.
The next day I went back to the pet shop
to pick them up.
When we got them home,
We put them into their cage.

Months passed…
and one thing that I noticed
was that they are different from each other.
One keeps making challenges for herself.
I wonder what they're doing just now.
Do you?

Mya MacRae

163

Catrina

One day my cousin got rushed into hospital.
She had a really serious disability.
She couldn't walk or talk or breathe properly.

A few weeks later her big sister was sleeping in the hospital.
Her mum was sleeping on the chair.
During the night Claire checked on Catrina.
She wasn't breathing.
She shouted on her mum.
The nurse came and checked her.
She told Claire she was dead.
Catrina's mum told my mum.
She told me and Stephanie.
We were really upset.
When it was her funeral, it was on a school day.
I said, 'I can't believe she is actually dead.'
I nearly started to cry because I was so so sad.
My friends asked me to cheer up and play, but I couldn't.
Just couldn't.
My mum and dad stopped at the school after the funeral
To see if I was okay.

Sometimes I wonder how she's doing in heaven.

Kayleigh MacRitchie

He aged 9

Has ginger hair that changes
colour when he has too much hair.

Has a cat that he loves so
much because it makes him
happy when he comes home.

Has a freckle in line with his nose.

Feels sad when his Dad says
'I'm in Spain and I'm living there forever.'

Has dry skin on the side of his face.

Hates most veg.

Has a Mum that he knows loves him loads.

Daniel McArthur

Erin-Bru

One Sunday morning, May 1st 2001,
It was twenty-seven days 'til my birthday.
My sister Erin was still mean to me,
Even though it was near my birthday.
She wouldn't let me watch TV.
I was so mad.
She told me to go and get her Irn-Bru.
I really didn't want to go.
So I didn't.
I got my bottle and filled it up to the top and came in.
She asked me, 'Where 's my Irn-Bru?'
I finally gave in – or did I? …
I gave her the Irn-Bru and sat near her.
'Perfect,' I whispered.
I climbed up on the couch.
I grabbed the Irn-Bru,
And I poured it over her head.
She screamed as it dripped!

Michael McCardie

She aged 9

She has very soft skin
Light green eyes
Quite a few freckles.
She is very kind.
Has black hair.
She loves fruit,
Except bananas and pears.
She is always happy if her friends are happy.
Loves playing with her Nintendo Wii.
Felt sad when she found out
her brother died three years before she was born.
She likes Maths and Drama.
Her favourite teachers are Mrs McCay and Mrs Park.

Caitlyn McColl

The Hill

Once I went to the park.
I took Kayleigh as well.
We took our bikes with us.
My Dad took his bike.
My Dad said, 'Come up the hill.'
I did.

I didn't know how to work my brakes.
I went up the hill.
My Dad came down the hill first.
I went down.
My Dad was shouting, 'PULL YOUR BRAKES!'
Then CRASH! BANG! BOSH!
'OOH!' I said.
I was screaming and crying.
I skinned my knees.

Tammy McFarlane

She aged 9

Has blue crystal eyes.
Loves animals, especially horses.
Loves art.
Feels happy when her friends are happy.
Feels sad when her friends are sad.
Has a freckle under her mouth.
Has three like a triangle on her nose.
Has a coo's lick on her fringe.
Loves Mrs McCay, Mrs Park and her friends.
Felt sad when her Gran died.
Loves
Her little
Brother.

Michaela McLeod

The Day I fell in Mud

One day I went to the animal safari park
On the elephant's 40th birthday.
After the party (I was about seven at that time)
Me and my family went to the pig farm to see the pigs.
I went over to one. The pig was coming
Towards me.
I was running away screaming
AHHHHH!
Then another pig came towards me.
I blinked. I opened my eyes. I was flat face
In the mud.

Andrew McWhinnie

The Tunnel

In the tunnel it was dark and dusty.
I took a step and kept falling until I hit the ground.
I stood up and I noticed a door, so I opened it.
On the other side of the door there was a blue light.
I closed the door then took a seat on the floor.
Suddenly I felt a streak of panic.
'I can't see the door,' I said in a whisper.
Suddenly I heard footsteps.
The door opened.
In came a fuzzy blue ball.
'I recognise you from somewhere,' I said.
'You probably do,' the fuzzy ball replied.
'I'm from your nightmares,' he said sounding chuffed.
Then he handed me over a bottle of anti-dream catcher.
Whilst he explained how to use it,
I noticed that the door was open, so I took my chance.
I gave him a punch on the nose and ran out of the room.

Zoe Rafferty

My Uncle dies

On November the fifth, my Uncle was not very well.
He had pain going down his back. My Mum said,
'Do you want me to call an ambulance?'
He said, 'No.'
'It will be better for you,' she said.
'Okay then,' he said.
My Mum called an ambulance.

A couple of weeks passed,
and he asked the whole family up to the hospital.
Me and my big brother went up on Sunday 21st of November.
He was drifting into a coma but we didn't know it.
On the Monday, my Mum got a phone call.
He died. I was so upset.

Kerry-Ann Reilly

Grandad 'died'

Grandad was not well.
He was in hospital.
We went to the hospital.
We went up to see him every day.
One day he was sleeping, but we thought
He had died.
He wasn't dead. He woke up.
We were over the moon.

Baillie Robertson

ASDA

It was Saturday.
My mum said,
'We've run out of milk. We have to go to ASDA.'
'Do we have to go?'
'Yes!'
I got depressed.
We went.
We just arrived in the shop.
My mum rushed right to the pans.
I thought, 'Here it goes.'
It was about thirty minutes.
We were just finishing.
My mum forgot something.
She told me just to wait beside the trolley.
I was waiting. Then I heard a big noise.
I ran as fast as I could.
I turned round and my mum had fallen right down.
Everybody came running over and said, 'Are you okay?'
She burst out laughing.
I was so embarrassed.

Struan Robertson

New Year's Day

On New Year's Day I went up to my gran's.
I was with my brothers – Paul, Daniel and my wee brother
Jack.
My mum was there with my dad too.
My cousin Craig was there.
My uncle Gary and my auntie Linda were there.
My gran made a buffet for us.
There were spicy chicken pieces.
Everybody was wanting them.
I said, 'I want them all!'
I was pushing everyone out of the road.
There were only five good bits.
Everyone was going for them.
I pushed my wee brother Jack away.
My big brother Paul was going for the last good bit.
He picked up the wrong one.
I slid across the floor.
I put my hand on the good bit.
I said when I got it, 'YES!'
I was going to take a bite.
I dropped it.

Jordan Stewart

The Prank Day

One day I wanted to prank my Dad.
Last April he said I was moving house.
The car broke down so we had to walk one mile.
Then he told me we weren't moving.
So I pranked him good, very good.
I got a glass of milk and I put butter on the milk bottle.
When he went to pour the milk on his cereal it slipped out
Of his hand. It smashed.

Sean Stone

Primary Six

She aged 10

Has black long hair.
Got a scar on the top of her right eyebrow.
Two brown eyes, dark as black.
Loves to draw.
Loves her baby brother's lovely face.
Hates boys, but not all.
Angry when Ben cries.
Sad when she thinks about China.
Happy when she plays with her friend.
Loves everything in school, teachers too.

Jia Ying Chen

My Journey

Step by step I walked down the ladders.
It was bright, shallow and it smelt like roses, and it was clean.
I opened the door and stepped inside.
There were chocolate bars, money and waterfalls.
I saw a white horse walk towards me.
I said to it 'What is your name?'
The horse said 'Snowflake.'
She pulled a present out.
I opened it.
It was a red rose.
I pulled out a present from my pocket and gave it to her.
It was a ribbon.
I turned round to go home.
She said to me before I went, 'Remember me.
I will always be in your mind,
and take some money for you and your family.'
So I took some money and I headed off,
and I knew I would never forget her.

Jodie Conroy

He aged 10

Has blue eyes.
Has dark eyebrows.
Has long eyelashes.
Has dark blonde hair.
Likes maths.
Likes P.E.
Likes football.
Likes basketball.
Doesn't like spelling.
Thinks his sister is a pest.

Aidan Docherty

My Tunnel

I was in a tunnel.
It was very dark.
I opened a door.
I was in a place called Chocolate Land.
Everything was covered in chocolate.
I saw a man and he said 'Hello and welcome.'
He gave me a chocolate crown and I gave him a diamond.
He said to me 'Please don't go.
You can be king of Chocolate Land!'

Brian Douglas

He aged three months

Has black small eyes.
Loves to fly.
Hates sitting in his cage.
Loves to look at himself.
Loves his tweety pie.
Has soft blue feathers.
Has cute wee feet.
Loves his swing.
Has a fine tweet.
Loves to make a mess.

He aged three months is my budgie, Joey.

Rachel Duncan

Mind World   by Ross Findlay

In the tunnel it was dark, wooden and dirty with lots of bugs.
All I could see for miles and miles was stairs.
At last I saw a spot of light under a large door.
I knocked on the door. It sprung open with a bang.
I walked out of the tunnel.
The daylight was so bright that it blinded me.
When a cloud covered the light I could see again.
I saw lots of trees, fountains and buildings.
I saw a bench so I walked over to it and sat on it. It was wet.
I felt like I was sitting there for hours.
I saw a man in the distance.
He had a man's body with horse's legs, blue skin
and a black beard.
He walked up to me.
I said 'What do you want from me?' But he said nothing.
He was holding a pole in his hand.
It was wrapped in gold foil. He gave it to me.
I opened it and inside there was a red golf club.
I looked up to him again
and I noticed he was wearing a checked golf cap.
I felt something hard in my pocket.
I took it out and looked at it.
I gave him the box. He opened it.
His face looked surprised.
It was a Rubik's Cube.
I turned round and walked away.
He shouted my name. I stopped and turned round.
He said 'May the golf club be with you.'
Then one second later he disappeared. I shrugged,
and walked back into the tunnel and back up all of the stairs.

He aged 10

Has black hair and has brown eyes.
Loves art.
Can touch his nose with his tongue.
Hates school sometimes.
Hates getting up in the morning.
Loves drawing.
Has two scars – one on the face and one on the belly.
Loves swimming, football, netball and sometimes golf.
Hates shopping.
Loves going on holidays.
Loves playing with his friends.

Ross Gallacher

She aged 10

Has brown hair that is always in a ponytail.
Has a scar on her nose
and one on her top lip too from when she was little.
Has discovered she likes reading poetry.
Has big brown eyes.
Has a freckle beside her nose and one on her chin.
Likes being in her friends' company.
Loves to laugh.
Feels sad when no one is there for her.
Feels angry when her sister gets her into trouble.
Has discovered she likes writing poetry.

Seana Garty

When my Gran went to the Beach in her Slippers

Once my Gran, my Gran's friend, my two cousins Beth and
Abby and me went on holiday.
First we had our breakfast.
We had eggs and sausages. It was mouth-watering.
We were full, so we went to the beach.
There was this really annoying old woman behind us
who had wooden sandals.
It was really annoying because they went clip, clop, clip, clop.
We got to the beach.
The sand was really warm.
We kept jumping up and down.
Finally, when we got to the sunbeds
I noticed Gran was wearing weird shoes.
She was wearing her slippers!
Me and my cousin started shouting at my Gran.
'Gran, you're wearing your slippers!'
'Oh! Yes, I am!' said my Gran.
Me and my cousins ran into the sea
and left my Gran wearing her fluffy purple slippers!

Alison Glass

The Flying Dog

One day we were tidying up my room.
Now, my dog is not allowed upstairs
because he gets fur all over the bed
and my brother is allergic to dog fur.
My Mum said 'Get the dog downstairs!'
So me being five and not knowing anything,
I flung him down the stairs!
I was in BIG trouble!!
Every time I stepped in the living room
my dog hid under the table.

Cameron Hannah

When my Gran's dog died

My Gran had a dog – Sasha.
She was old.
She didn't eat for about two weeks.
I often stay with my Gran.
When I get out of bed I always walk down the stairs.
Sasha my Gran's dog is always there smiling.
I was staying at my house.
Then I went over to my Gran's house the next day
and asked 'Where is Sasha?'
She said 'She's up in heaven.'
Straight away I burst into tears.
I was going to go out and she said 'WAIT!'
She went into the room and brought out Sasha's leash.
Then she said 'Take Sasha's leash' and I burst into tears!!

Brian Hepburn

The Time that my Dad took off his Shirt in Town

Once I went to town with my mum and dad.
My dad went to a shop to get a new shirt.
After, when he got his shirt, he sat on a bench.
I was standing about ten inches away from him.
He took his old shirt off.
I couldn't stop laughing.
A woman said to me,
'Is there something wrong with you, son?'
I said to her 'Wouldn't you be bursting out laughing if your
dad took off his shirt in town?
Then my dad put on his new shirt.
We saw the woman again.
She could not let go of her laughter.

Daniel Kennedy

Journey

I walked down the dark scary tunnel.
It took me ages to get down loads of stairs.
I felt tired when the stairs were done.

I saw a door, so I opened it.
I arrived in my bedroom.
The TV was on as if I was welcomed.
I sat on the bed and I watched TV.

My Dad came.
He was the special person I was meant to meet.
He was dressed in a white cloak.
His hair was the way it used to be.

He gave me a present. It was a cuddle.
I gave him a gold chain.
He said 'Love you! Look after your Mum.'
I said 'Don't go please. I'll miss you.'

Sasha Kerr

The Door

I walked down the tunnel. It was very dark.
Had lots of stairs.
It was *very* scary.

I arrived at the beach.
With Gold skies.
The sand was quicksand.

I saw my imaginary friend, Alvin.
He gave me a gold watch.
I gave him a chew toy.
When he was leaving he said 'Oo ah!'
Then he walked into the horizon.

Aidan Lynch

Lucky Dip   by David Marshall

One day my class started a fundraiser for a charity.
Then we picked a group.
The groups were lucky dip, badge it, hair beading,
beat the goalie, pin the patch on Pudsey, art competition,
guess the name of the teddy, bring and buy and a bakery.
I chose lucky dip.
First we had to design a poster.
Me, Brian D and Billie-Jo (my group) started quickly.
Most of it we found easy.
Then on the day before we had to get ready.
Yip, we had to wrap the prizes – this took HOURS!
We had the idea that I would get the tape
and they would wrap the prizes.
When we got about half way, we got help.
It still took a lot of time. Finally we got it done.
Once everyone came in, we got a lot of people.
Then the Janitor paid us to do the lucky dip. We did it.
I got a lot of pencils.
I thought Why not sell them?
We put them in three bundles
and sold them for twenty pence each. EASY MONEY!
When we sold about a third a little kid looked
and then just took one.
Other people started to do it too.
This got REALLY ANNOYING!
After everyone left we got to go to the other stalls.
I won a book about David Beckham (I never read it once).
I also bought a small cake – it was delicious.
At the end I donated my left-over money to my group.
I really enjoyed that day.

Birthday Fight

On my birthday my Mum let me have my birthday party at
Bellahouston.
I asked most of my class to come and all of my family.
It was ready for all my family and friends to come.
They all came.
After they all came we played tons of games like pin the tail
on the donkey, hide'n' seek, and snakes and ladders.
After a while I got bored so I sneaked up to my cousin Claire.
I threw a ball at her. (It was very soft!)
She threw a ball at me.
It missed!
It hit my friend James!
'BALL FIGHT!' shouted James.
The birthday fight began.
Finally the ball fight ended. It lasted for an hour.
We had birthday cake and some food.
They all left.
I told my Mum 'This was the best party EVER!'

James Marshall

Yesterday

Yesterday Siobhan bought my friend a Valentine's card.
He said 'I'll open it tomorrow.'
He went with me to my house
but he was behind me opening the card.
I said 'She'll go mad!'
He said 'It's mine!'
I got my dinner.
Then we went outside.
We saw Siobhan and we ran down to her
and he went mad!
She told on him.
Then he ripped the Valentine's card.
Siobhan went mad.
So Sean had to run!

Dylan McColl

193

The Loch Ness Monster Game

One day me and my big brother were playing a game
called the Loch Ness Monster Game.
What you have to do is put a quilt over you
and try to catch the other person.
My brother Sam went first.
Sam caught me, so I was 'it'.
I heard him in one direction
so I ran and jumped and banged into a wall.
I started crying but he was laughing.
Then my Dad came in and shouted
'SAM GET TO YOUR ROOM!'
I had a big lump and sat in the living room.
It was bedtime but I could not go to bed
because I had just bumped my head.

Courtney McCrear

He aged 10

Has realised his eyes are blue.
Has found out he likes basketball a lot.
Has found out that reading is fun.
Feels sad when he is alone.
Feels happy when people are there.
He likes to laugh.
He likes to be active.
He likes it when people care for him
rather than pretending he isn't there.
He realised his hair is brown and that he has freckles.

Josh McDonald

Another Dimension

I saw ten other tunnels that were wide.
I walked into one and saw a field with loads of trees and a
lake.
I walked over to the lake and got a drink.
I saw a reflection of a dragon, eight foot tall and giant wings.
He gave me a knight.
He had gold armour, a mace and a shield with a dragon logo.
I gave him a pair of trousers and shoes.
Then he just walked away and faded into the trees.

Grant McGaffin

She aged 10

Has green-brown eyes.
Has brown curly hair.
Loves to dance.
Loves music.
Thinks about a special person.
Loves having sleepovers.
Loves to laugh.
Loves playing with friends.
Loves dogs.
Loves being happy.
Loves watching Mean Girls.
Hates when her sister annoys her.

Megan McGinty

Fester the Dog aged Twelve

She aged twelve is called Fester.
She aged twelve has beautiful soft golden hair.
She aged twelve has lovely brown eyes.
She aged twelve has little white paws.
She aged twelve is the best pet I could have.

Jordana McGlinchey

Onion Rings

One day I went to a very posh restaurant.
We sat down at a table.
The waitress came over to take our order.
I ordered roast chicken with gravy.
The waitress came over to give us the meal.
My Mum and Dad got onion rings.
I got to have one.
It was gooey and slimey.
I spat it out!
'OOOOOOOOOOOOOOHHH!!!'
It was horrible!
It was …
SQUID!!!
I ran to the toilet.
I was sick in the toilet.

Carly McGuire

The Day my Grandad died

One day me and my Gran were going to Govan.
My Grandad was going to take a shower.
When we came back my Gran shouted on my Grandad
to tell him we were back.
My Grandad never answered her.
She tried again but he still never answered.
My Gran went into the bathroom.
My Grandad was lying there.
My Gran shouted on my uncle David.
My uncle David ran down the stairs.
My Gran told him to call 999.
My Gran dragged my Grandad into the bedroom.
She looked out the window.
The ambulance was there.
My Gran ran out and told them to hurry up.
When the man and woman came in
the man dropped his bag and all the stuff came out of it.
They took forever to clean it up.
My Gran was shouting at the woman to help my Grandad
but when they got to my Grandad it was too late.

Zoe McKechnie

200

The Surprise Limo

On my birthday some of my friends came to my house.
I thought my Mum was dropping them off in her car.
A while later my Mum said to me
'Close your eyes and go outside.'
I went outside and there was a PINK LIMO!
I was jumping up and down.
The others were laughing.
I said 'What are you laughing at?'
They said 'We already knew!'
I laughed.
Inside the limo were black leather seats.
It was fantastic!

Toni McMahon

My Bumped Head

Once when I was two my Mum had a cabinet.
I was learning how to walk
with my Mum and Dad at either side of me.
I walked towards the cabinet.
I tried to walk to my Dad and SMASH!
I had bashed my head on the cabinet.
My Dad was rushing and shouting.
My Mum was nearly crying.
My Mum picked up the phone calling the hospital.
'COME QUICK!'
The ambulance came very quick and she was crying by then.
My Dad was saying 'MY DAUGHTER IS GETTING HER
PICTURES DONE NEXT WEEK!'

The next week flew in.
It came to the day I was finally getting my pictures done
and the bump went down.
I got my pictures done.
The picture with me lying down – I had a scar on my head.

I was angry at my Mum when I was older.

Emma Mitchell

My Ninth Birthday

When I was nine my Mum came to my room. I was asleep.
My Mum said 'Wake up.'
I said 'Why are you waking me up?'
My Mum said 'Ooh! It's your birthday!'
I started jumping on my bed.
When I got to the sitting room everyone said
'HAPPY BIRTHDAY!'
Everyone brought a present for me.
My Mum gave me clothes.
My aunt gave me some sweets.
Everyone was happy.
After the celebration we went for dinner.
'This is your best birthday' said Mum.
I started enjoying dinner.

Aysha Mwanyali

My Journey in the Park

I was in the park with my friends.
I saw a gold door.
I opened it.
It was cold, dark and grassy and had lots of stairs.
At the end of the stairs there was another door.
I went in the door.
It was like a desert, sandy and hot.
I met a little mouse.
She said 'What's your name?'
I said 'My name is Billie Jo. What's your name?'
She said 'My name is Louise.'
She gave me a present.
Her babies.
I gave her some food.
She said 'Don't go please!'
I said 'I have to! Bye!'

Billie Jo Revie

The Fire Pot

One day my cousin told me to put oil in the pot.
I went to put oil in the pot.
I came to the room.
I forgot about the pot.
My two cousins forgot about it too.
My cousin Safia was busy watching TV.
My other cousin Jahid was busy talking on the phone.
Suddenly it was the fire alarm.
We went to look at what happened.
There was a fire.
My two cousins ran to the kitchen.
My cousin Safia saw the oil was on fire.
She was trying to stop it with water.
My cousin Jahid was screaming and jumping up
because it wouldn't stop.
Jahid said 'Okay okay okay I will stop.'
I was laughing and jumping up.
My Father came.
My cousin Jahid told my Father.
He gave me trouble.
I was still laughing because of my cousin.

Salma Safi

205

My Tunnel

My tunnel was very wide.
It had lots and lots of stairs.
It was bright pink with decorations.
I went through a door and came out at a beach.
There was a chocolate fountain.
I saw seagulls.
There were people in the water.
I saw a lovely blue dolphin.
It said to me 'Hello and welcome to my beach.'
The dolphin gave me a present.
I opened it. I was surprised. It was a surfing suit.
The dolphin said 'Jump on my back.'
I had a present for the dolphin.
I had five fish to give to her.
I didn't have any idea I had fish in my pocket.
The dolphin was sad when I was walking away.
She shouted 'Siobhan please don't go. You're my friend!'
I said 'I'm sorry but I can't stay any longer.
It's nearly my dinner time.'
Mum said 'Where were you?'
I said 'You wouldn't believe it. I was talking to a dolphin!'
She said 'None of that nonsense again.'

Siobhan Trivett

The Adventure

The tunnel was a dark, dirty, tight space.
There were lots of stairs.
Finally I got to a door, a wooden door. I opened it ...
It was a beach, a lovely beach.
I could see miles of beautiful calm water,
And beautiful soft sand.
I could hear the water splash.
Then I saw a girl.
Her name was to be Sharon.
What a lovely name.
She pulled out a package.
It was for me.
I opened it ... a beautiful gold ring!
But I didn't have anything for her.
Then I pulled out a present for her.
I gave her perfume.
It was time for me to go.
Then I heard her shout my name.
'AMY!' she called.
What was her message?
'You were the greatest friend I ever had!
So can't you stay?'

Amy Weir

Primary Seven

Ready to kill

I was at my friend's house.
We were playing on the trampoline.
We were playing a game called 'Last Man Standing'.
You have to make everyone fall.
I had just to make everyone fall.
I had just won my third game in a row
when my little brother came.
He asked if he could play.
He came on and we started playing.
My friend went out first.
Now it was me and Jack.
Brother and sister, ready to kill.
I flew forward and lunged at him.
He tried to get away but I was too quick.
I grabbed his wrist and threw him.
He went, bum, belly, bum, belly.
He lay there sprawled over the trampoline.
I bent down.
I heard him breathing. Great! He wasn't dead.
Then I heard a snigger.
I looked down. It was him.
I was raging.

Amy Boyle

Berries

At Blairvadach
on the first day we got introduced to our instructor Rob.
Later that day we went on a small hill walk
on the hills at Loch Long.
It was a great adventure.
We walked up past a small cottage
and scrambled up steep slopes.
About half way up we stopped for a view.
Amy, Jodaine and Kiera started picking up
these small round things, thinking that they were berries.
The instructor came up and said
'That's not berries. That's POO!'
The joke then stayed with our group for the whole week.
We kept on reminding them.

Ross Bradley

Evil Dog and Boy

Where I stay there was a dog that always barked at everyone
Until one day a boy was walking.
The dog ran up behind him and barked at him.
The boy turned round and kicked the dog.
The dog was never seen again.

Robert Brown

Stuck in the Mud

When we went to Blairvadach we went burn bashing.
We went to the beach.
We started skimming stones.
We had to go back. We were running out of time.
On the way back we came across a swamp.
Me, Vicky, Kiera, Amy B and Jodaine decided
we would go in.
It was very deep. We were sinking right into it.
We screamed 'Help!'
Me and Amy B got ourselves out.
Vicky, Kiera and Jodaine could not get out.
They were in too deep.
They had to get the instructor to pull them out.
He got Kiera and Vicky out.
Jordaine was stuck. She had gone too deep.
After five minutes he pulled her out.
It turned out quite funny.
The mud was half way up our wellies.
We all got hosed down.
Finally we got a shower.
I was glad about that.

Amy Carlin

The Suitcase

One day we went to Blairvadach.
When I got there it was time to unpack.
There was a problem. I couldn't open my case.
Some friends tried to help me.
Then I got a teacher. She couldn't open it either.
We took it down the stairs.
We all got called to the lobby, where we hang out.
One of the instructors opened my case with a screwdriver.

Jodaine Copeland

My Sleepover   by Chloe Cumberland

It was my birthday and my mum decided to have a sleepover
for me later. She asked all my friends to come round.
For my birthday one of the things my mum bought me was
duvet covers for my bedroom. I really liked the covers and I
asked my mum if she could put them on at the sleepover.
'Okay,' she said. 'Just don't get chocolate or juice or
anything over them.' 'Okay,' I said.
Later my friends came round.
One of my friends had a nose bleed problem since she was a
baby.
My covers were on and all of us were carrying on.
Megan, the girl with the bleed problem started annoying me.
She wouldn't stop!
I could feel the anger filling up inside me.
I couldn't control myself.
I turned around and punched her right on the nose, and blood
went EVERYWHERE! Including my covers. OH NO!
Megan started screaming and crying.
My mum started walking up the hall
shouting 'What's wrong?'
'Err … nothing. Go away. Everything's fine.'
'Well it doesn't sound fine to me.'
I was holding the door shut and I was trying to clean up the
blood at the same time while my mum was trying to open the
door.
Eventually she got the door open, and she saw all the blood.
Oh no, I thought. Mum please don't give me trouble.
'It's okay,' she said. 'I'll give them a wash.'
My mum took Megan into the bathroom and cleaned her up.
Afterwards we all watched TV, ate chocolate and drank juice.
Everything was fine.

Dog Run!!

In primary 4 we went on the Glasgow bus tour.
We were having a break.
All the class were waiting about.
Then this dog came.
We all went to clap it.
It started coming after us.
We all started screaming 'Help!'
We ran for our life.
It was scary.
Sean was last in the line.
The dog was running really fast and bit Sean.
He was crying.
The teacher made sure he was okay.
He was. It was just a little sting.
The teacher told us all to go on the bus and forget about it.
No one could forget.
We were all really scared.

Vicky Evans

When Amanda bumped her Face

One day I was out playing with my friend Amanda.
We were playing hide and seek with everyone around my bit.
We were running.
She slipped on a banana skin.
She got up and started laughing.
Everybody was gob-smacked.
Her face was bleeding.
She got up and went in the house.

Kayleigh Flavell

Crazy Sleepover

For my 11th birthday I went bowling at the Quay.
Hollie, Jamie and Heather were invited.
After we had gone bowling
they all came to my house for a sleepover.
We sorted out all the beds and where everyone was going to
sleep.
We were all watching Harry Potter.
Then I noticed that Heather had fallen asleep.
So I turned off the TV.
We all started whispering crazy things into her ear.
Then she started saying them in her sleep!
It was really funny.
So we decided to take it a step further.
We started speaking French to her
And she copied us.
She was even attacking my bed!

Then Heather woke up!
She didn't know what was going on.
We told her what she'd been doing.
She thought she had gone absolutely bonkers!

Colette Gibbons

The Roadworks

It was summer. My friend came round to my house.
My mum asked if I could go to the shops.
So I did.
Me and my friend were making our way to the shops.
At the top of the street, there were roadworks.
I told her 'Look out for the ...'
Before I could say 'roadworks' she fell down the hole
head first.
She started to scream and shout 'Help!'
I pulled her legs. She was out and on the pavement
full of mud.
I was trying not to laugh at her going to her house.
She got changed and cleaned up.
Finally we got to the shops.
Then we went back to my house.

Beth Glass

My Flying Bike

One day I was on my bike.
I was dropping my cousin off at the bus stop.
The bus came. She drove away on the bus.
We were on our bikes.
Up ahead there was a big ramp.
I thought to myself, 'I am going up that ramp.'
I did. I went flying through the air. I felt scared.
Finally the bike touched the ground.
The front wheel of the bike came off.
My chin hit the ground.
I burst my chin wide open.
I have still got the scar today.

Richard Haggarty

My Best Shoes

When I was a baby my mum and dad got my shoes.
They were so nice.
I had them when I was one day old.

My wee cousin came up.
She was playing with them and she had a pen in her hand.
I said 'You try and I will kill you. I got them when I was one
day old.'
I went to tell my mum. It was too late. She did it.
I was so so mad with her.
'I am going to kill you.'
She said 'No you will not. If you try it I will ring 999.
You are a wee beep.'

Andi Keaney

Herny Kinerny*

One day last year I went to Kelburn Country Park.
I went with my mum, dad, sister Jade and her friend Brooke.
I was so excited.
I went on a horse. It was called Chip.
Jade and Brooke also went on a horse.
All of a sudden Chip took a hairy canary.
He ran about mad.
I was nearly off the horse.
I fell off Chip and he ran over me.
I was bursting out crying.
After that I went on another horse.

* A herny kinerny or hairy canary = a fit

Hollie Masson

Down the Stairs

When I was seven years old I loved Superman.
I always wanted to be like him.
When I was watching a Superman movie
I couldn't take it any more.
I needed to be like him.
I got a cover and a couple of pillows.
I put them in a bunch at the top of the stairs.

The first time I didn't really move.
The second time I got some more pillows
and pushed off from the wall.
I still didn't move.
I started thinking I was never going to move.
Then out of nowhere my sister jumped out
and scared me so much
that I fell backwards on to the covers.
'Ahhhhhhhhh!' I screamed.
The cover and I started to move!
I went down the stairs!

The next day I thanked my sister and asked her
never to do that again.

Sean McCardie

My Hamster

When I was eight I had a hamster.
His name was Squeaky. He was brown and white.
One day my cousins came over. They are older than me.
They took Squeaky out and he ran away
and my cat chased him and gobbled him up.
My cousins started laughing. I kicked them in the privates.
They were screaming their heads off.
Then I started laughing and told all my friends after they went home.
They were laughing and did not touch my pets again.

Darren McGaffin

Camping Bed!

When I stayed at my old house,
my cousin Allan was staying with me.
The morning after he was lying in his bed.
But it wasn't a normal bed.
Ohhh No! It was a camping bed.
I had woken up.
I ran into the living room (where Allan was sleeping).
I thought,
'I'm going to jump on him to wake him up and to annoy him.'
I jumped on his stomach
He woke up
I felt a spring in the bed pop
I suddenly jumped up
I sat on the couch as fast as I could
I looked round
The bed had closed right up the middle
With Allan still in the bed!
He shouted 'Kiera, I'm going to kill you!'
I then shouted 'It wasn't me!'

Kiera McGuire

Soup

When we were at Blairvadach
We got soup.
It was disgusting.

The next day we were on a hill walk.
We walked past a river and it was copper-orange.
It was like the soup that we had for dinner the night before.
I felt sick.

Scott Mersey

Our Lesson

One day at school Mrs McCay taught us a poem
called 'The Lesson.'
The poem is about an older brother
who tries to trick his younger brother to jump down the stairs
and fall.
That day Hollie was coming to my house after school.
We were bored.
We decided to act the poem out.
Hollie went to the top of the stairs.
I waited at the bottom.
I counted to five – '1,2,3,4,5.'
Hollie jumped to the bottom and fell.
We both laughed!

Carley Mullen

The Carnival

One Saturday I went to the carnival.
I went with my friend and her mum and dad.
I had never been on any rides before.
So I never wanted to go on any.
My friend's mum Nicole said that I would at least go
on one ride before we went home.
The first ride I went on was the drop zone.
I was waiting in the line.
I hoped it would hurry up.
Then it was my turn.
I wished I was at the end of the line now.
I was so scared.
It started to move up, and up, and up, until …
it dropped.
I had butterflies in my tummy.
When I got off
I said 'Can I go on again?'

Katie Murphy

Smokey and the Box

One day me and my family had to take my pet cat Smokey
to the vet.
We had to take him to get his jags.
We had never taken him to the vet before.
We thought it would be easy.
We were totally wrong.
The day before we had bought a pet box from the pet store.
We brought the pet box into the living room.
Some of his nuts that he eats were in the box.
We left a trail leading to it.
Smokey followed the trail of nuts, eating every one of them,
except the ones inside the box.
Then we tried to push him into the box.
He just kept on biting and scratching us.
'YOU'D BETTER GET IN THERE YOU STUPID CAT!'
raged my dad.
Suddenly my dad busted the cage door open
and shoved the cat right in!
Then once the cat was in
We realised that the box was too small.
Then it just burst open and Smokey jumped onto my bed,
AND WENT TO SLEEP!

Calum Robertson

Saving Hollie's Life!!

Hollie and I went to our cheerleading show.
Hollie likes to chew plastic.
She was chewing the plastic off her water bottle.
She swallowed the plastic by accident.
She was coughing and coughing.
I was patting her back for ten minutes really hard,
then sick came up.
The plastic was free from Hollie's throat.

Jamie Thomson

Scott's Disaster

One day me, Scott and Vicky went a walk around the block.
They were having dinner with me.
We went a walk because we were bored.
We were walking round the corner.
These boys stopped Scott and said 'Hey I know you.'
'No you don't' replied Scott.
Me and Vicky just kept walking
thinking Scott would follow us.
But as we turned around,
we saw Scott lying at the side of the road.
We ran back and helped Scott up.
He had hurt his leg.
We had to help him back to my house.
As we got in, dinner was ready.
Once we finished dinner
We just stayed in and played with my rabbit.

Hayley Wright

For other titles from Augur Press
please visit

www.augurpress.com

Printed in the United Kingdom
by Lightning Source UK Ltd.
134376UK00001B/122/P